The Unity Factor

One Lord, One Church, One Mission

JOHN H. ARMSTRONG

Foreword by Timothy F. George

Christian's LIBRARY PRESS

GRAND RAPIDS · MICHIGAN

The Unity Factor

© 2011 by Acton Institute

Used by permission of Christian's Library Press.

Cover image: Mandala of 12 Hands © Kycstudio
Source: www.istockphoto.com

ISBN 10: 1-880595-90-7
ISBN 13: 978-1-880595-90-9

Library of Congress Cataloging-in-Publication Data

Armstrong, John H.
    The Unity Factor / Armstrong, John H.

CHRISTIAN'S LIBRARY PRESS
*An imprint of the Acton Institute
for the Study of Religion & Liberty*
161 Ottawa Avenue, NW, Suite 301
Grand Rapids, Michigan 49503
Phone: 616.454.3080
Fax: 616.454.9454
www.clpress.com

Copy edited by Jan M. Ortiz
Cover design by Peter Ho
Interior composition by Judy Schafer

Printed in the United States of America

For the advancement of the missional mandate of Jesus Christ in the third millennium and the renewal of biblical ecumenism through the witness of the Holy Scriptures and the wisdom of the Christian tradition.

For my friend Dr. Stephen Grabill and the ministry of the Acton Institute, a fellowship of people who practice the kind of ecumenism that is making a major contribution for Christ and his kingdom.

CONTENTS

FOREWORD

Great things in the kingdom of God often arise from small beginnings—an insignificant mustard seed yields a mighty crop, some kid's leftover lunch feeds a hungry crowd, a small candle on a stand floods the whole room with light. Thus began the quest for Christian unity in modern times. A poor journeyman shoemaker, William Carey by name, traveled to India to share the Good News of Jesus Christ with those who had never heard it. Carey was a Baptist, but he soon realized that he needed the encouragement and support of other Jesus-followers (Christians) in order to fulfill his mission.

Carey called for a gathering of great commission Christians to come together, pray together, and work together on a coordinated strategy for world evangelization. Carey called for this meeting to take place in 1810. While nothing came of Carey's "pleasing dream," as he called it, the idea did not die. Exactly one hundred years later, the International Missionary Conference was convened in Edinburgh and two hundred years later, the Third Lausanne Congress on World Evangelization took place in Cape Town, South Africa. The modern quest for Christian unity was born on the mission field. Its aim was not the building of a supra-ecclesiastical bureaucracy but rather the unhindered declaration of Jesus Christ, the sole and sufficient Savior of the World.

This book by John Armstrong stands in the tradition of William Carey, Edinburgh 1910, and the Lausanne Conference at Cape Town 2010. It is a gospel-focused and Scripture-based summons for all believers who stand in the great tradition of Christian faith and life to love one another so that the world might see and know that Jesus Christ is Lord. It is a call for Christian believers of all denominations to demonstrate their love for one another by following Jesus together. May God use this appeal to awaken in us a Carey-like faith in fulfillment of Jesus' great prayer for his disciples found in John 17:

> The goal is for all of them to become one heart and mind—
> Just as you, Father, are in me and I in you,
> So they might be one heart and mind with us.
> Then the world might believe that you, in fact, sent me.
> The same glory you gave me, I gave them,
> So they'll be as unified and together as we are—
> I in them and you in me.
> Then they'll be mature in this oneness,
> And give the godless world evidence
> That you've sent me and loved them
> In the same way you've loved me.* (vv. 20–23 [MSG])

—Timothy George

---

* Eugene Peterson's *The Message*.

INTRODUCTION

Christians are called to unity in love *and* to unity in truth. This affirmation is self-evident in the New Testament. Visible unity contributed mightily to the holistic mission of Christ in the first two centuries of the Christian era. Today, all across the globe, a rising tide of voices urges us once again to make unity a priority in the work and witness of the church. The principle that prompts this collective call is *the unity factor*. The unity factor means that all of us must do our part to contribute to a full-orbed expression of the Christian oneness that we inherently share because of the Holy Spirit. This expression of oneness needs to happen in a fresh, Spirit-given way that we have not seen since the first centuries of the Christian church.

The renewal of all Christian believers should lead us to pursue a *distinct* response to the unity factor. This response will come about when we recognize the three "ones": *First, one Lord.* We will recognize that there is only one Lord—Jesus of Nazareth—the anointed one of God, the Messiah (Christ). *Second, one church.* We will see afresh that there is only one church—the Spirit-given community of Christ's entire global body. The members of this one church are united through the Holy Spirit in his love. Thus, we must work to express what already exists in the triune purpose of God. *Third, one mission.* The one church exists by and for the singular mission of Jesus in the world. The call and vision that I share constitute a biblical and practical way of working out the unity factor.

The 1996 *Evangelical Manifesto* put this vision in simple words:

> In this day … [the] critical need for unity and godliness among Christians is being met with a surging desire for just such a transformation. And, it is springing up across the breadth of the church. It could well be that the body of Christ is ready now to allow the pastoral prayer of the Son of God in John 17:20–23 to renew itself dramatically in our lives.[1]

The Earliest Christians

It is an established fact that the earliest Christians disagreed with one another. The New Testament makes that abundantly clear. Some of these disagreements profoundly threatened the unity of the church in its infancy. The book of Acts shows how Christians resolved disagreements in the midst of a rapidly growing church and mission (Acts 15:1–35). In fact, it is in the context of a divided local church that Paul gave us the clearest of all tests for determining whether the Holy Spirit is actually present. "Therefore I want you to know that no one who is speaking by the Spirit of God says, 'Jesus be cursed,' and no one can say, 'Jesus is Lord,' except by the Holy Spirit" (1 Cor. 12:3). Some have suggested that the phrase *Jesus is Lord* was the earliest creed of the church. It surely was the shortest. However, do not let the brevity of these three words fool you. What these words are saying is amazing. The way to discern whether or not an individual is speaking from God is to listen carefully to what

---

1. National Association of Evangelicals: *An Evangelical Manifesto,* 1996, 2002.

they say about Jesus. Yes, false teachers might repeat certain words, but soon enough their lives will reveal that Jesus is not central to who they are.

Christians have always realized that truth is found in a person (John 14:6), not in a philosophy: Jesus is Lord. Thus, his life, death, burial, resurrection, ascension, and return are central to what this confession means. There is no disagreement about this; all Christians believe that there is one Lord—"and he [Jesus] will reign for ever and ever" (Rev. 11:15).

Jesus also taught his disciples that he would form a church (the word *church* literally means an assembly of people): "I tell you that you are Peter [which means 'rock'], and on this rock I will build my church, and the gates of Hades will not overcome it" (Matt. 16:18). Peter's confession that Jesus is Lord was revealed to him by God. Jesus says that upon this apostle, and upon his confession that Jesus is Lord, Christ will build his church. Note that Christ clearly says: "I will build my church." If we understand what Jesus says here, we will realize that all *our* efforts to build the church are misplaced. We obey Jesus; we love Jesus; and we give witness to Jesus' love for the world, but we cannot *build* his church. Our calling is to confess him as Lord and "work out [our] salvation" (Phil. 2:12) in a living community of his people (Eph. 2:19).

Make no mistake. Christians have variously understood the meaning of the word *church* down through the ages. They have even debated what constitutes a church. What are the marks and signs of the church? Or, to put it another way, what is essential to its DNA? Some scholars believe that distinct differences among Christian communities (churches) existed from the beginning even though the one church of Jesus remained united, broadly speaking, for at least several centuries.

We know that just moments before the risen Jesus ascended to the Father, he said to his disciples: "You will receive power when the Holy Spirit comes on you; and you will be my witnesses in Jerusalem, and in all Judea and Samaria, and to the ends of the earth" (Acts 1:8). Note carefully that he says, "You [my disciples] will be my witnesses." This is not an imperative as much as it is a statement about the result of his power. Jesus preached the kingdom of God, the reign of the Messiah (Matt. 6:33; 12:28; 19:24; Mark 1:14–15; 10:15; Luke 4:43; 6:20; 8:1; 9:2, 11; John 3:3, 5). He also taught his disciples to pray that his kingdom would come on earth as it is in heaven (Matt. 6:10). The way to make his kingdom known to the ends of the earth is through faithful witness, a witness that often includes persecution and martyrdom. True witnesses (*witness* is our English word *martyr*) bear faithful testimony to the transforming power of Jesus. Good witnesses can share only the news they know from experience. Furthermore, through such witnesses the mission of Jesus soon became central to the life of the earliest Christians. To varying degrees, and in spite of frequent failures, this has remained true down through the ages. Christians have universally believed that Christ gave his followers a mission to be pursued in obedience through the power of the Holy Spirit. They know they must make this "hope of glory" (Col. 1:27) known by their witness and mission.

However, what has prompted a faithful response by Christians? Recent biblical confessions, adopted by global Christian leaders, have expressed what seems patently clear in Scripture: "We love God because God first loved us."[2] God's great love motivates us (2 Cor. 5:14). Only the power of a vital relationship with Jesus will prompt Christian love and biblical martyrdom.

We must understand that the mission of Christ flows directly from the love of God. Thus, the mission of Christ's church flows through our love for God and expresses God's love for the whole world. *The Cape Town Commitment* adds, "Comprehensive

---

2. *The Cape Town Commitment: A Confession of Faith and a Call to Action*, The Third Lausanne Congress (Peabody, MA: Hendrickson, 2011), 9.

biblical love should be the defining identity and hallmark of disciples of Jesus."[3]

This *comprehensive biblical love is the defining identity and hallmark* of all true followers of Jesus. I believe this is the central truth we must recover if we want the world to take notice of our witness. Today, the world mocks much of what we say and do. A great deal of this is deserved. This, however, was not the case in the earliest centuries of the church. Christians' deep sense of shared, familial love led them to love even more deeply. As our present world polarizes politically and socially, the church must refuse to follow the ways of the world, returning instead to this unity factor. This is *the* truth that will allow the world to believe that the Father sent the Son in order to save it (John 17:20–23). This is our greatest defense for life-changing faith. Arguments designed to answer skeptical questions or emotional reactions aimed at the postmodern rejection of the biblical narrative will not fundamentally change anyone. There is a greater and better way—the way of love (1 Cor. 13).

The Defining Identity of the Disciples of Jesus

The New Testament writers use many names and metaphors to describe the church. For example, the body of Christ, the household of God, a royal priesthood, disciples, Christians, followers of the Way, servants, flock, wife, bride, and so forth. Whatever else we may say about the church, we can agree that the church is the people of God in Jesus Christ. It is not first an organization and then a people. It most certainly is not a building. A simple reading of the New Testament shows that Christ's church (people) exists *both* universally and locally. It is *both* a vast multitude (on earth as well as in the presence of the ascended Christ) and a local gathering of redeemed people who, through his grace, worship the living God. Indeed, the church is

---

3. *The Cape Town Commitment*, 10.

a living and worshiping multitude that extends back across time and forward into all eternity. God's truth stands firm: "The Lord knows those who are his" (2 Tim. 2:19).

What distinctly marks those who belong to Christ? What truly distinguishes them from those who are *not* the church in this present age? It is not a cluster of doctrinal beliefs, as important as beliefs and doctrines are for healthy religious life. It is not a label or a particular social marker. Rather, is not the true mark of the church love? Furthermore, is not this love both Christ's love for his flock and their love for their shepherd and one another?

Love for Christ is, in a profound way, *the defining mark* of true Christians (1 John 3:11, 14, 16–18, 23). We can ask a myriad of questions about our own profession of faith in Christ. However, at the end of the day, it comes down to the same question Jesus asked Peter: "Simon, son of John, do you love me?" (John 21:15–17).

This has nothing to do with what you have done for Christ or for the cause of religion. It has little to do with your gifts or your sacrifices for God. However, it is a simple and life-changing question: *Do you love Jesus?* When Jesus questioned Peter three times about his loyalty, Peter answered, "Lord, you know all things; you know that I love you" (John 21:17).

Many times I have doubted my own profession of faith in Christ, which I first made when I was only a young boy. I have failed him more than I care to admit. My private thoughts have accused me, and my sinful and doubting heart has often been prone to wander far from God. I have sinned in thought, word, and deed far too much to ever think too highly of my profession.

At such times, I have been brought back to John 6, where I read that many of Jesus' disciples began to leave him. They said of his teaching: "This is a hard teaching. Who can accept it?" (John 6:60). However, Jesus actually turned up the heat, and even more people began to leave, at which point he asked the Twelve: "You do not want to leave too, do you?" (John 6:67). Simon Peter, answering for the group, provides the answer that I have used so many times in my journey: "Lord, to whom shall we go? You have the words of eternal life. We have come to believe and to know that you are the Holy One of God" (John 6:68–69).

If we belong to Christ, then we *are* his disciples. Disciples take up the cross daily and follow him along a path of self-denial, service, and obedience. Jesus promises his Spirit to those who come to him in love. "If you love me, keep my commands" (John 14:15). Although we are not perfect, not by any stretch, we daily purpose to follow him and happily flee to him for grace and mercy each time we fall.

Therefore, I believe that the indelible mark of Christians is perfectly clear. We love him, and this truly shows that we are his followers. Because we love him, we love one another: "We love because he first loved us" (1 John 4:19). This puts my simple point into clear perspective. Jesus loves us. He pours his love into our hearts, and as a result, we love one another. This is the *core* of the unity factor.

As I mentioned in the beginning, the unity factor is established by three ones—one Lord, one church, and one mission. In the following chapters, we will look at each of these in detail to see if this claim is true.

1

ONE LORD

One of the most impressive developments over the last one hundred years of Christian history has been the tendency of churches and Christians of different traditions and ethnic backgrounds to draw closer together. There is a growing concern to create an open space where Christians from a broad range of churches and missions can confess Jesus Christ as perfect in his divinity and humanity. The more global the church becomes, the more this is happening. We are discovering that the world is smaller than we thought. In some places, where the church was once dominant and strong, we now see decline and weakness. Here Christians are beginning to realize that they need one another more than they ever realized. This discovery is helping many to see that the church is much bigger than they thought. This is why I titled a book I wrote *Your Church Is Too Small* (2010). I did not mean that your local church or your particular church family or tradition is too small. I meant that your concept of the church is too limited by human factors. These factors hinder your ability to see the reality and importance of the whole church in your community or to the global church around the world.

Earlier I noted that the first creed used by the earliest Christians might well be found in Paul's brief statement "Jesus is Lord" (1 Cor. 12:3). Some things in the Bible baffle the best scholars. However, this truth—Jesus Christ is Lord!—is clear to all who have eyes to see and ears to hear.

> You know the message God sent to the people of Israel, announcing the good news of peace through Jesus Christ, who is Lord of all. (Acts 10:36)

> If you declare with your mouth, "Jesus is Lord," and believe in your heart that God raised him from the dead, you will be saved. For it is with your heart that you believe and are justified, and it is with your mouth that you profess your faith and are saved. (Rom. 10:9–10)

> Yet for us there is but one God, the Father, from whom all things came and for whom we live; and there is but one Lord, Jesus Christ, through whom all things came and through whom we live. (1 Cor. 8:6)

> There is one body and one Spirit, just as you were called to one hope when you were called; one Lord, one faith, one baptism; one God and Father of all, who is over all and through all and in all. (Eph. 4:4–6)

> Just as you received Christ Jesus as Lord, continue to live your lives in him. (Col. 2:6)

Christians in the first century had no written creed. This does not mean, however, that the earliest Christians had no distinctive beliefs until centuries later. In fact, the most basic of all Christian beliefs was confessed long before there was any creed. The New Testament reveals this one truth beyond any reasonable doubt. Distinctive beliefs were critical for the development of the early church, especially in the face of pagan and polytheistic religions. However, the distinctive belief was that Jesus was the one Lord. If you think about this, you will soon realize how preposterous this claim was to people in the pre-Christian era. This must be why the apostle Paul said the message of Jesus and his cross was "foolishness" to both Jews and Greeks, prompting many to say that it was sheer nonsense (1 Cor. 1:23–24).

By the second and third centuries, Christians began to compose concise summaries of their faith to be used at their baptisms and when they gathered for worship. These summaries became the basic material for the first and second great creeds of the early church—the Apostles' Creed and the Nicene Creed. The word *credo*, from which we get our word creed, means, "I believe." It was necessary for Christians to explain what their confession of "Jesus is Lord" really meant. It was also necessary that they teach (catechize) those who wanted to understand the faith.

Jesus had clearly commanded his disciples to teach "them to obey everything I have commanded you" (Matt. 28:20). Thus, Jesus gave the church a curriculum. All the commands that he gave to his disciples, eventually encompassed in the Holy Scriptures, were to be obeyed. Note again the connection here to obedience. We like to stress that teaching is an end in itself, but Jesus said there was something to be understood *and then obeyed*.

2

ONE CHURCH

If you are Christ's disciple, I hope to convince you of the greatest life-changing discovery of my Christian life. I hope to do this in extremely simple language. I know the risk of brevity is great, but I am willing to take that risk to help you see that this one truly big idea is linked to three biblical truths that flow out of our love for Jesus. If your desire is to defend what you already know, to protect your comfortable box, then there is very little that I can do to change your mind. However, if you have followed me to this point, I must believe that you are open to seeing more clearly.

I Pray That They Will All Be One

Several decades ago, I was the pastor of a local church where I had begun preaching through the entire Gospel of John. I rather meticulously preached from each chapter and verse for several years. Sometimes I covered longer sections, and sometimes, as with John 3:16, I preached several sermons on just one verse.

As I came to the end of my twenty-year-pastoral ministry, I faced my final Sunday. The text before me was John 17:20–23.

I thought I understood this text, but the more I wrestled with it the more it transformed me. Jesus said:

> My prayer is not for them alone. I pray also for those who will believe in me through their message, that all of them may be one, Father, just as you are in me and I am in you. May they also be in us so that the world may believe that you have sent me. I have given them the glory that you gave me, that they may be one as we are one—I in them and you in me—so that they may be brought to complete unity. Then the world will know that you sent me and have loved them even as you have loved me.

I had read this text countless times. I had a built-in sense of what it meant and was quite sure what it did not mean. I was sure that it had absolutely nothing to do with what is commonly called ecumenism. This big word refers to the efforts made by various Christians and their leaders for greater Christian unity or cooperation. The word comes from a Greek word that means "the whole inhabited earth." In ancient times, it referred to the councils that were convened to preserve the unity of the church through careful statements of central doctrines. In modern times, the word is used predominantly with reference to Christian denominations and churches separated by doctrine, history, and practice. Thus, the term *ecumenism* refers to the idea of Christian unity as both a local and a global initiative. It might have bad connotations for some readers, but, in itself, it is a wonderful word.

As I read John 17 more carefully, I could not escape the truth of what Jesus was asking the Father. He prayed for the oneness of all his followers. This is indisputable. Imagine, the Son of God, on the last evening before his death, prayed that all Christians in all eras of all time would love one another and experience unity.

The New Commandment

This section of John's Gospel is sometimes called "the book of glory," with good reason. After a prologue in John 1:1–18 the author gives us what becomes "the book of signs" in 1:19–12:50. Then the writer says that to all those who accept him Jesus will reveal his glory by returning to the Father in the hour of his crucifixion, resurrection, and ascension (13:1–20:29). Fully glorified, he will then give the Spirit to his followers.[1]

This glory is framed by what Jesus calls "the new commandment."

> When he was gone, Jesus said, "Now the Son of Man is glorified and God is glorified in him. If God is glorified in him, God will glorify the Son in himself, and will glorify him at once.
>
> "My children, I will be with you only a little longer. You will look for me, and just as I told the Jews, so I tell you now: Where I am going, you cannot come.
>
> "A new command I give you: Love one another. As I have loved you, so you must love one another. By this everyone will know that you are my disciples, if you love one another." (John 13:31–35)

Perhaps the most obvious thing that you notice when first reading this text is that love for others is not really a new commandment. Leviticus 19:18 says, "Do not seek revenge or bear a grudge against anyone among your people, but love your neighbor as yourself. I am the LORD." God had commanded love for one's neighbor centuries before Jesus came in the flesh.

So, what is *new* about this commandment? The answer is so obvious that there should be no debate. Jesus is saying that the love he wants his disciples to express for one another is based

---

1. Raymond F. Brown, *An Introduction to the Gospel of John* (New York: Doubleday, 2003), 298.

on his dramatic displays of deep love for them—displays that are rooted in his deep love for the Father.

At this point, we have to ask, "How did Jesus love his Father?" The answer from Jesus is this: "I love the Father and do exactly what my Father has commanded me" (John 14:31).

Jesus' love for God was expressed by perfect obedience within the unique relationship that he had with his Father, a relationship rooted in divine love. Now this same (divine) love is what he gives to us. He then commands us to follow this love throughout this age. He promises to send his Spirit to empower all his disciples to love in this same manner (John 14:15–31).

A Relational Love

The love that Jesus desires for us, according to the new commandment, is clearly one of relationship. The love Jesus enjoyed with his Father is the same love that he gave to his disciples so they could live in him until the end. This love was intensely spiritual, but it was bound up with the whole human person of each one of his followers. Jesus did not love his disciples in some vague or generic manner but rather completely, fully, and to the very end. His love was relational, not nonmaterial or unseen. In fact, one could say that his was the love of deep friendship.

I have come to believe, over the course of six-plus decades of life, that this love is not difficult. In fact, it is utterly impossible! We cannot love as Jesus loved unless we have the life-giving power of Jesus working in us through the energy of the Holy Spirit. Thus, this will not happen if we are unwilling to obey him as he commanded us. When we fall in love with him, we can love as he loved.

Be honest. Your actions matter a great deal. They matter to you and to those touched by your life. How you react to other people really matters, because your actions will reveal the identity of the true God to those who do not know him. The only Jesus that most people will ever see is the one they see in you.

The only way they can see this Jesus, who deeply loves them, is on the basis of your relationship with other Christians in a context in which the world sees God's love as they witness the new commandment being lived out.

We need to be honest about this. We Christians have given the world an ugly caricature of God. As a result, multitudes cannot hear our good news. They hear us shouting at one another and stridently attacking one another's views and actions. They know already that we oppose their lifestyle, and they feel condemned by us. A plethora of studies reveals this sad fact all too plainly.

A surprise bestseller, *Unchristian: What a New Generation Really Thinks about Christianity … and Why It Matters*, gathered insights from adults who spanned a wide array of ages and traditions. It explained how modern people really see us. Words such as *hypocritical*, *antihomosexual*, *sheltered*, *too political*, and *judgmental* jump out at the reader.[2]

I humbly propose that what Jesus clearly intended for us can be understood in these two words: *relational love*. We understand this even more clearly when we read his prayer for unity carefully.

The Oneness He Desires

From the very beginning, the Christian church has thought of itself as one, not two, three, or four. This is not accidental.

Ephesians 4:4 says that there is "one body." I still remember where I was and what I was thinking when the force of this statement hit me. I had always said, "Yes, there *is* one spiritual body, but there are many churches and denominations." I even argued that this was a good thing because it brought about an immense diversity in the mission of Christ. I concluded that the oneness referred to in Ephesians 4 had no *real* bearing on *how*

---

2. David Kinnaman, Gabe Lyons, and Lloyd James, *Unchristian: What a New Generation Really Thinks about Christianity … and Why It Matters* (Grand Rapids: Baker, 2007).

I lived or *how* my church functioned in our local community with regard to other Christian churches.

However, a moment came when the words *one body* gripped my soul profoundly. The word *one* would not let go of me. There was not my church and your church but Christ's one church. This church is God's family and a holy temple for the Lord. It is the body of Christ. This is the bride that Jesus gave his life to redeem, and he wants this whole church to live as one because he cherishes it and cares for it.

In this same epistle, Paul highlights the fact that this one church has a central place in the eternal plan of Jesus Christ for the whole world (Eph. 2:14–3:13). God's design was to unite divided peoples (Jews and Gentiles) into one new group, the church (1:9; 2:14–22; 3:6). For Paul, the church was a community of those who submitted to the lordship of Jesus (5:21–24) according to God's eternal purpose of bringing everything in heaven and on earth together under Christ's reign (1:9–10). The church comprises people from every ethnic group and is a community of peace where believers live together in love, bound by their baptism and their shared experience of the Spirit (Eph. 4:2–6). Does this sound like what you see in your community of faith?

The church is to be a showcase of grace. Here the world should be able to see what it means to forgive, to be reconciled in love, and to pursue the unity of the Spirit in peace. I was reminded of this recently while on a visit to Rome. I realized that in pre-Christian Rome, religion, mercy, and forgiveness were *not* virtues. Only by the power of the Christian faith did a wholly new understanding of virtue begin to revolutionize culture.

Most of what I have just said I believed from the day I began public ministry as a church planter more than forty years ago. However, as a good individualistic American Christian leader, I thought ministry was primarily about my private life and the fellowship of my own congregation. I knew I needed to love everyone in my congregation (that itself seemed impossible), and I knew that the members of my congregation needed to love one another. What I did not know was what all this love had to do with other Christians or churches around me. They did their work, and we did ours. That was as far as my understanding of oneness went.

One Holy Catholic and Apostolic Church

Some of you have recited the words of two of the best-known ancient creeds. Others may not have recited these creeds, but you know them, and all of you should believe them if you understand them.

The Apostles' Creed says the Holy Spirit calls us to be "one, holy [and] catholic." The word *one* was taken directly from statements such as Ephesians 4:4. There is only one Christian church. The word *holy* was taken from a plethora of biblical texts that call the people of God to be distinct from those around them. Both morally and spiritually, the church is to be unique. The word *catholic* literally means "throughout the whole world." It is an ancient way of saying that the church is global. On the basis of this word, we can speak of catholicity as a quality or state of universality, which reminds us of the comprehensive nature of the church. The word *apostolic* (added by the Nicene Creed) roots the church in the doctrine and life of the apostles. The church is historic and should be measured by the teaching and witness of the apostles, not by the fads of the time.

These four words—*one, holy, catholic,* and *apostolic*—have been called the classical marks of the Christian church. They provide a perspective for our life together. They also provide a broad but strong basis for our common understanding of what it means to be the church in every age.

The creeds place these four words in a stanza that addresses the ministry of the Holy Spirit. This is not by accident. Paul says in 1 Corinthians 12:13, "We were all baptized by one Spirit so as to form one body—whether Jews or Gentiles, slave or free—and we were all given the one Spirit to drink."

19

When I was baptized, it was not as a Baptist but as a Christian. There is not a Baptist baptism, a Reformed baptism, a Pentecostal baptism, a Methodist baptism, a Lutheran baptism, a Catholic baptism, or an Orthodox baptism. There is only Christ's baptism. In fact, the only meaningful label that will likely remain in the new heavens and the new earth is *Christian*.

Do you really think that your denominational and/or church label is important? In the tenth and eleventh centuries, when the Western and Eastern Churches broke apart under mutual anathemas and excommunications, there was a rise of various new groups of Christians. It has been said that there were several evangelical groups in the West during that period of time. These groups included the Petrobrusians, the Henricians, the Arnoldists, the Humiliati, the Taborites, the Waldenses, the Lollards, and the Bohemian Brethren. However, where are these today, at least in terms of denominational identity? I suspect that most people have heard of no more than one or two of these groups. Nevertheless, they broke fellowship over various issues and created something similar to our modern denominations. If Jesus does not return for another five hundred years, will our modern labels matter? Will they be footnotes in history's texts? There is growing evidence to suggest that this might be the case.

Please do not misunderstand. The diversity of each church can contribute powerfully to the health of the whole church. However, this diversity should not lead to new schism. Can there be diversity *and* unity? The answer in the New Testament seems clearly to be in the affirmative. We must understand that unity is not singing in unison and losing all our distinctiveness; unity is singing in harmony in a way that allows each person and tradition to enrich the others.

The nature and definition of the church have been discussed and debated from the beginning. There is nothing I, or any other writer, can say that will unite us in one common way of understanding the church. We can make no progress at all if we refuse to confess that before the throne of Jesus himself there is only one church—his church. No matter what your claim is about your church being a visible and faithful church, you must acknowledge that all the people of God are not *all* found within your church.

The late theologian John Leith wrote: "The church exists where the Word of God is heard in faith and obeyed in love."[3] I think most of us can agree that this is a starting place. There will remain many things to discuss if we are to reach greater expressions of visible unity, but if we begin here, we start at the center. We begin with Christ and work within relationships of love where we can find agreement.

3. John Leith, *The Church: A Believing Fellowship* (Atlanta: John Knox, 1981), 21.

3

ONE MISSION

Both the New Testament and the earliest creeds indicate that God is one God. This one God is Father, Son, and Holy Spirit. Although the New Testament does not use the term *Trinity*, the doctrine is so apparent in Scripture that faithful Christians employed the word to explain what they encountered in knowing Jesus and the teaching of the apostles.

The early Christians had an overwhelming experience of this man Jesus and of the activity of God in their midst through him. As they followed the ascended Jesus, they talked a great deal about what his life and teaching meant. They believed the ancient biblical words "Hear, O Israel: The LORD our God, the LORD is one" (Deut. 6:4). This verse can be translated in several ways, but the central thrust is clear: God is one; and there is no other God but the Lord, the God of Abraham, Isaac, and Jacob. He is the Most High, the Creator, and the true and only Lord.

Believing that God was one God, not three gods, these followers of Christ remained equally convinced that there was no other way to explain Jesus but to receive him as Lord; that is, as fully God. Thus, they asked, "Are there two Gods?" They affirmed that there was only one. So then, was Jesus the same as the God of Israel? Not exactly. Jesus called the God of Israel his Father. This is why the earliest creeds are divided into three stanzas. The first is devoted to what the church believed about the Father, the second to what they believed about the Son, and the third to what they believed about the Holy Spirit. However, the creed does not end with a simple mention of the Holy Spirit as a person who is fully God. The Nicene Creed adds: "We believe in one holy catholic and apostolic church. We acknowledge one baptism for the remission of sins. We look for the resurrection of the dead, and the life of the world to come. Amen."

The Creed thus emphasizes the activity of the Spirit rather than the inner being of the Spirit. Everything in this final statement has to do with action. For example, the connection of the Holy Spirit with the forgiveness of our sins is crucial. The Spirit is much more than one of the names we are baptized into as Christians. The Spirit initiates us into the Spirit-filled community of Jesus and gives us the experience and reality of our forgiveness in Christ.

Christian churches have differed in their *emphasis* about the experiences we have with the Holy Spirit. The Catholic, Orthodox, Anglican, and Lutheran traditions have all stressed the Spirit's role in acting through the sacraments of the church. The Reformed tradition, so far as it has followed Calvin's teaching, has also seen the Spirit's work in similar ways. The Pentecostal tradition reminds us that the Spirit works particularly in the gifts and powers bestowed on the faithful. However, one thing is common to all Christian traditions—the Holy Spirit is given to empower us for Christ's mission.

The Cape Town Commitment, cited at the beginning, states this so powerfully:

> We love the Holy Spirit within the Trinity, along with God the Father and God the Son. He is the missionary Spirit sent by the missionary Father and the missionary Son, breathing life and power into God's missionary Church. We love and

pray for the presence of the Holy Spirit because without the witness of the Spirit of Christ, our own witness is futile. Without the convicting work of the Spirit, our preaching is in vain. Without the gifts, guidance and power of the Spirit, our mission is mere human effort. And without the fruit of the Spirit, our unattractive lives cannot reflect the beauty of the gospel.[1]

The Global Church

We have been afforded an amazing opportunity in the twenty-first century. The world is getting smaller and smaller, and people are becoming more deeply connected as their ideas and lives converge in a way that could never have been possible only a few decades ago. Ease of travel, the flow of goods and people, and the social network all make the world much smaller. There is serious debate about what all this means, but there can be no doubt that we are going through a revolution that will likely have deeper consequences than the Industrial Revolution, which radically remade the world in the eighteenth and nineteenth centuries. The consequences of this new revolution will last for centuries and leave the world a very different place from what we have known in history. The twenty-first century is seeing a great transformation. The question for Christians remains: "What shape and expression will our faith take in this new cultural and social context?"

---

1. *The Cape Town Commitment*, 15.

4

WHAT DOES THE UNITY FACTOR LOOK LIKE?

For more than forty years, I followed what I was taught as a young Christian regarding the church and its mission. I believed that there was one church but this one church was (primarily) invisible. The true church was unified in the truth—and I knew the truth. If you were a "real" Christian (and I often thought I knew who these people were and were not), then you were in this invisible church. If you were not "born again," then it did not really matter what visible church you belonged to because you were not a real Christian. This led me to separate myself from many excellent Christians and churches because they were not "biblical" like me.

In 1994, I sat in a church where the Apostles' Creed was affirmed in worship. I will never forget the overwhelming sense of God's presence that I experienced when I felt the weight of these words: "I believe in one holy catholic church." I had preached from John 17:20–23 just two years before, and the truth of this text had been disturbing me deeply. It seemed that everywhere I turned I saw little evidence that unity mattered to most Christians. I was quite sure the unity Jesus prayed for had to be visible and intensely relational. Let me explain.

In John 17:21, Jesus clearly prayed for the unity of his followers through all ages ("for those who will believe in me" [17:20]). When Jesus' followers are one, then it is possible "that the world may believe that you [the Father] have sent me" (17:21). If this unity is invisible, then how can the world see and believe that the Father sent the Son? No amount of retreating and reinterpreting would allow me to escape this question.

Then we read, "I have given them the glory that you gave me, that they may be one as we are one—I in them and you in me—so that they may be brought to complete unity. Then the world will know that you sent me and have loved them even as you have loved me" (John 17:22–23).

Jesus prays for our "perfect unity." Some versions translate Jesus' prayer for us as "being brought to complete unity" or becoming "completely one." No matter how we read it, Jesus desires that all believers be united in working for his glory in the world. He desires our unity in his mission.

Sometimes it is quite hard for North American Christians to hear the words of Jesus clearly. Our cultural and doctrinal assumptions, often intermingled in ways we do not understand, hinder our seeing and hearing. I discovered a rich insight into Jesus' prayer for our unity from an African leader. His cultural and ethnic context speaks into our own with considerable clarity, showing that our struggle with obedience to the unity factor is *not* just an American problem.

> Unity may be defined as the condition in which something forms an organic whole. Although different elements are involved, the whole is characterized by agreement and internal coherence. This definition applies to the unity of believers to the extent that they share a common foundation of faith and practice. While the word *unity* may be rarely used in the Bible, the idea of unity is often found.

In the nations and villages of Africa, unity is also strongly dependent on family ties, on the use of a common language, or on the fact of living in the same geographical region. This unity is vulnerable because anyone who comes from another area or who does not speak the same language is perceived as an outsider, or even an enemy. Hence, there is no unity involving all the nations of the region.

In Israel, as in Africa, unity could only be partial, limited to one nation or one close-knit community. But in the New Testament, there is an unlimited, universal dimension to the unity of believers. This unity knows no geographic, administrative or cultural limits. It is based in Jesus. By his death and resurrection, Jesus opened the way to new alliances for all peoples.… Through faith in Jesus, the believer is part of a new nation, reconciled to God and capable of living in genuine fellowship, a visible unity.

[This unity must be evident in the local church,] but the local church is only one link in the unity of the universal church. The unity that God brings extends to all believers of all nations, denominations and times. Tribalism, ethnicity and denominationalism are hindrances to the unity of God's people and must be resisted. Of course, each ethnic group or tribe has its place in the church, but only as links in a long chain. There is no place for ideologies that consider one ethnic group or tribe superior to another. Similarly, individual churches belong to different denominations, but this division must not be allowed to be an obstacle to unity and be defended on the basis of protecting church doctrine or by arguing that separation from others is the will of God.

Unfortunately, the unity that is presented in God's word has not yet been fully realized. Believers must be disciplined and built up by the word in order to come to maturity and arrive at visible unity. They must also support and maintain this unity through united efforts in such areas as mission and evangelism.[1]

---

1. Kuzuli Kossé, "Unity of Believers," an article in *Africa Bible Commentary*, ed. Tokunboh Adeyemo (Grand Rapids: Zondervan, 2006).

This African brother has expressed the unity factor powerfully. Just as I am sure that there is only one Lord and one church, I am equally sure that Jesus has only one mission. *The Cape Town Commitment* expresses the church's role with regard to this one mission very succinctly:

> Jesus calls all his disciples together to be *one family among the nations, a reconciled fellowship in which all sinful barriers are broken down through his reconciling grace.* This Church is a community of grace, obedience and love in the communion of the Holy Spirit, in which the glorious attributes of God and gracious characteristics of Christ are reflected and God's multi-colored wisdom is displayed. *As the most vivid present expression of the kingdom of God, the Church is the community of the reconciled who no longer live for themselves, but for the Savior who loved them and gave himself for them* (italics mine).[2]

A person who is a baptized follower of Jesus, who loves him above all others, is a Christian. (I have no right or responsibility to run a private detection service that seeks to determine who is and is not a "real" Christian.) Thus, a Christian belongs to the one church of Jesus Christ. What should we make of all these varieties of churches and groups that we now have? If my own family had a huge argument and we separated from one another, with some of us even changing our names in the process, how many Armstrong families would there really be? Well, you would still have a single Armstrong family acting like it was three or four very different families. Because the church is one family, it is under immediate obligation to discover every way possible to stop the family schisms and heal our myriad divisions. This means that we must strategically resist what John Stott called

---

2. *The Cape Town Commitment*, 26–27.

"our pathological tendency to fragment."[3] This seems so clear as to be beyond reasonable doubt.

Therefore, what was I to do with this clear teaching about unity in Christ's mission once it was so powerfully revealed to me more than a decade ago?

Rediscovering God

There are times in all our lives when we meet God in unusual ways. We often do not see these moments coming. There is a mystery about God and how he communicates with us in such moments. However, when powerful eternal reality meets us in the person of Jesus, we know that this is not something we manufactured. The Spirit is clearly at work—God is opening our eyes and ears in a new way. When I began to understand the unity factor with my heart, I knew I had to change. God was asking me, "What will you do with this great truth that I have shown you?"

As I grew more deeply into this vision of Jesus and his people, I also began to understand the centrality of the Trinity. This allowed me to see the need for both unity and diversity. I understood that God was a relational Being who exists in eternally intimate harmony. Each of the three persons perfectly relates to the other in love. The excellence of God's divine nature is beyond any ability that I have to comprehend it. I am sure of this: Eternal love is the very nature of God because "God is love" (1 John 4:8).

When God created humankind, he created us, male and female, to live in harmony with him and one another. He created us for unity. However, sin broke this unity and separated us from God and one another. The result of this separation has led to the destruction of people, marriages, families, and nations. Whole civilizations have fallen because of disunity and

3. John R. W. Stott, *Evangelical Truth* (Leicester, England: InterVarsity Press, 1999), 141.

separation. Furthermore, when humans have tried to restore unity on their own ideological and political terms, the result has almost always been to make things worse (Gen. 11:1–9).

Rediscovering the Good News of the Kingdom

As I have shown, the central theme of the Bible is Jesus. Jesus came to call people to be his disciples "[from] every nation, tribe, language and people" (Rev. 14:6). He calls them by his Spirit, through the good news of the gospel, into the communion of the church. P. T. Forsyth, a famous theologian who lived more than a century ago, rightly said, "The unity of the church lies not in itself but in its message, in the unity of the gospel that made the church."

The gospel that specifically called the church into existence is the gospel of the kingdom (cf. Matt. 4:23; 5:3; 6:10; Mark 1:14–15; 4:11, 26, 30; 9:47; Luke 4:42–43; 6:20; John 3:3, 5). This kingdom is God's reign. What is promised to the church in the New Testament is *not* the kingdom but the Holy Spirit whose presence gives witness to the kingdom; to the reign of God. The Spirit thus leads the church into the fullness of truth by keeping the church alive within the love and power of Jesus.

When the church recovers the centrality of the gospel of the kingdom, it will cease to think of itself as the end of Christ's mission but rather as the means to a much greater end—the missional kingdom of Christ. In the New Testament, a local church did *not* exist as an end in itself. Each congregation existed for the whole church, and the whole church existed to serve the kingdom of Jesus in a town, a city, and a region. Jesus commanded his disciples to pray, "Your kingdom come." He also told them to "seek first his kingdom." He expected his kingdom would have a profound influence in the world. (The parables speak of its largeness and eventual growth.) Through fear and misinformation, I believe we have very often missed the centrality of this kingdom message. We limit its expression to our institutional church, thereby treating other churches and Christian leaders as our competition. Even where we have stressed the gospel of the kingdom, we have stressed the individual and personal aspects of it rather than the *corporate* and communal. Further, we have concentrated on the moral and spiritual aspects to the virtual exclusion of the material and physical. This had led most Western Christians to divide life into activities that are seen as *secular* and *sacred*. Our preoccupation with ourselves has kept us from seeing that the gospel is about Christ's reign, not my personal satisfaction and success.

We must recenter our lives on the incarnate person of Jesus Christ who is the essential character of true unity. This is why his prayer for our unity in John 17 is so closely linked with his mission in John 20:21: "As the Father has sent me, I am sending you."

How did the Father send Jesus? He came in weakness, in profound humiliation, and as a man who was subjected to all temptation. He was, in short, completely vulnerable and deeply relational. He was even called "a friend of tax collectors and sinners" (Matt. 11:19). In the most relational and intimate of all contexts, he called his closest disciples his "friends" (John 15:14).

What defines the relational identity of Christians is the Incarnation; that is, God's taking on human flesh and dwelling among us in grace and peace. It is this incarnational identity that defines the oneness of the church Jesus prayed for in John 17. I believe this is the key to understanding the unity factor. The indwelling presence of the Holy Spirit empowers our oneness, making it real in our actual life experience. The gospel of mercy and forgiveness becomes the essential truth of our unity, the truth that holds us together in mission. As *The Cape Town Commitment* put it, "The core of our identity is our passion for the biblical good news of the saving work of God through Jesus Christ. We are united by our experience of the grace of God in the gospel and by our motivation to make the gospel of grace known to the ends of the earth by every possible means."[4]

---

4. *The Cape Town Commitment*, 23.

As the Father Sent Me, So I Send You:
An Incarnational Mission

The three primary texts I have taken from John's Gospel eventually framed my life-changing discovery of the unity factor. The first is John 13:34–35, where we see the new commandment. The second is John 17:20–23, where we see Jesus' prayer for our unity in relational love. The love that the incarnate Christ shared in his relationship with the Father was to be the same love I shared in with other Christians. We reach maturity in this love, not by holding precisely the same views on every matter we consider but rather by learning to trust one another and live in Christ's abiding love. The unity we experience is organic, not organizational. Maybe nothing is more frequently misunderstood by those who seek to apply the unity factor to real human contexts. The third text that shaped my understanding of the unity factor is John 20:21: "Again [Jesus] said, 'Peace be with you. As the Father has sent me, so I am sending you.'"

God sent Jesus into the world to establish his kingdom. Now Jesus sends us, his disciples (the entire church), into the world in order to carry out the mission of his kingdom. This is the same truth previously given in John 17 in the context of Christ's prayer for our visible unity. "As you sent me into the world, I have sent them into the world" (John 17:18). Christ sets us apart to be his sent ones. Sent by him, we are a sending, missional people.

How was Jesus sent into the world? He was sent as a person filled with the Holy Spirit and set apart for the kingdom of God. He lived in communion with the Father and always obeyed him. He was the only man who ever lived in perfect communion with God by the fullness of the Holy Spirit. We do not live perfectly, as he did, but we can live faithfully in his mission by the power of the same Spirit.

We must grasp the fact that Jesus sent his disciples into the world, not as soloists, but as members of a community chorus. He sent them out of their comfort zones into a place of challenge and distraction. He sent them out in groups, as friends. This is the principle of incarnation and community. This is kingdom mission.

Because of this understanding, a new term—*missional*—has caught on. Whereas mission is something the church does, and missionaries are people sent on a particular mission, the word *missional* refers to the inner reality of "sentness" shared by all Christians together. As the three persons in the Trinity are involved in the sending mission of God, the church is sent because the sending God is reaching into the whole world to announce the reign of Christ through the good news of grace. The word *missional* underscores the truth of John 20:21. Christopher Wright says:

> Mission is and always has been God's before it becomes ours. The whole Bible presents a God of missional activity, from his purposeful, goal-oriented act of creation to the completion of his cosmic mission in the redemption of the whole of creation—a new heaven and a new earth.[5]

Our challenge is to move mission from a budget issue to the center of our life together. We must understand what Swiss theologian Emil Brunner said in the twentieth century: "The church exists by mission as fire exists by burning." When a local church becomes missional, it becomes a who-based ministry that releases leaders and people to activate the skills and strategy of the whole community. North American Christians have lived on formulaic mission for more than a century, and the consequences are deadly, as summarized in the oft-repeated statement "The American church is three thousand miles wide and an inch deep." The missional church will carefully discern its core commitments and value its shared mission above maintenance and sending dollars to causes far away. Theologian Craig Van Gelder has expressed this well:

---

5. Christopher Wright, "An Upside-Down World," *Christianity Today* 51 (January 2007), 45.

The church is more than what meets the eye. It is more than a set of well-managed functions. It is more than another human organization. The church lives in the world as a human enterprise, but it is also the called and redeemed people of God. It is a people of God who are created by the Spirit to live as a missionary community.[6]

Missional-Ecumenism

As I sought to embrace the vision God gave me of the unity factor, I came to use a hyphenated term that expressed this vision succinctly: *missional-ecumenism*.

In this term, I express two great truths that came together in my understanding. First, God is, in himself, perfect unity. As a perfect, loving, giving, and sending God, the Father, Son, and Holy Spirit are deeply and personally involved in saving the world. Mission is God's *before* it is ever ours. We must reconnect mission with God's being and activity in the world before it can rightly become our work of making disciples. If we fail this priority, we will not accomplish Christ's mission in the twenty-first century.

Second, the Father's desire is that all those who follow the Son, by and through the Spirit, will be relationally one with him in his sending mission. Through this relationship, we will become one with each other in the process of obeying and doing the mission that Jesus gave to the whole (catholic) church. Mission is not so much the prerogative of each of us privately but of all of us together. This does not excuse us from our individual parts, but it does underscore that our individual parts cannot be detached from the whole if we follow God's missional design.

We cannot demonstrate to the world that the Father sent the Son (John 17:23) or prove to the world that we are the disciples of the living and reigning Jesus (John 13:35) unless we live in

---

6. Craig Van Gelder, *The Essence of the Church: A Community Created by the Spirit* (Grand Rapids: Baker, 2000), 24–25.

love and unity as his people engaged together in his mission as his sent ones (John 20:21).

Our Moment

The Cape Town Commitment states my own conclusion: "A divided church has no message for the divided world."[7]

Our failure to live the shared life that I have called missional-ecumenism is *not* a minor problem that we can ignore for another day. It is a "major obstacle" that hinders us in ways that we do not begin to comprehend. The problem in the West is evident. Our blindness is profound, and the cancer of our schism grows.

The world has come to our shores and found the witness of the church divided and ineffective. Even the newer, growing ethnic churches are badly divided. As powerful as the Korean witness has been to America, to cite one example that I know firsthand, the Korean witness is terribly divided into myriad groups and ideologies that compete for converts and causes. This happens when we pursue our agenda, mistaking our plans for Christ's. We assume all is well if our particular church or movement is gaining numerically. (The problem, however, is quite evident—every major expression of the church in North America is declining, and numerous studies have found that only one in ten churches is growing.) The church in the West continues to languish in spiritual poverty, yet we keep acting as if our mission is strong and our witness effective. *The Cape Town Commitment* addressed this problem succinctly:

> Partnership in mission is not only about efficiency. It is the strategic and practical outworking of our shared submission to Jesus Christ as Lord. Too often we have engaged in mission in ways that prioritize and preserve our own identities (ethnic, denominational, theological, etc.), and have failed to submit our passions and preferences to our one Lord and

---

7. *The Cape Town Commitment*, 65.

Master. The supremacy and centrality of Christ in our mission must be more than a confession of faith; it must govern our strategy, practice and unity.[8]

Unity is not only about new grassroots efforts that will help us work together. Grassroots solutions are double-edged. They can come out of the minds of individual activists who actually make things worse than they were before they applied their solutions. Biblical scholar Oscar Cullman believed that what we desperately needed was a "unity through multiplicity, through diversity." This is what I advocate. This idea prompted Pope Benedict XVI to write:

> Certainly division is harmful, especially when it leads to enmity and an impoverishment of Christian witness. But if the poison of hostility is slowly removed from the division, and if, through mutual acceptance, diversity leads no longer to mere impoverishment but rather to a new wealth of listening and understanding, then during the transition to unity division can become a *felix culpa*, a happy fault, even before it is completely healed.[9]

The history of past attempts at ecumenism is mixed. Parts of the larger agenda are still fiercely debated, often for good reason. Therefore, missional-ecumenism must never become a fuzzy niceness that fosters theological compromise. This call to a practical, community-based expression of our inherent unity in Christ's one mission cannot be put on the shelf. We need a mind-set that does not think concern for unity always leads to compromise. Real unity encourages diversity within the essential truths of the ancient faith. The stakes are too high for Christ's kingdom in the modern world for us to continue as if we safely live within a Christendom-based culture.

---

8. *The Cape Town Commitment*, 66.

9. Pope Benedict XVI, *Church, Ecumenism and Politics* (San Francisco: Ignatius Press, 2008), 135.

5

NOW WHAT?

Three times in John's Gospel Jesus repeated, "A new command I give you: Love one another. As I have loved you, so you must love one another" (John 13:34; see also 15:12, 17). Three times Jesus prayed that all his followers "may be one, Father, just as you are in me and I am in you" (John 17:21). Both the command and the prayer are missional. "By this everyone will know that you are my disciples, if you love one another" (John 13:35). Additionally, "I in them and you in me—so that they may be brought to complete unity. Then the world will know that you sent me and have loved them even as you have loved me" (John 17:23).

When people encounter the unity factor, one of the first responses I receive is, "But *how* do we do this?" The answer to this question is not to be found in a program. It is found in discovering what the Spirit is doing in your life, church, and community. I can offer scores of illustrations of how the unity factor is working across America and beyond. I devote an entire chapter of my book *Your Church Is Too Small: Why Unity in Christ's Mission Is Vital to the Future of the Church*, to illustrate this.

How does a pastor, business leader, skilled professional, hard-working laborer, or a busy homemaker actually pursue this vision? In other words, "What difference does it make to believe in the unity factor?" If I offered a simple answer, and truthfully, there is not one, you might be inclined to adopt a program and then miss the incredible journey that awaits you if you humbly welcome this vision of unity. For me, the journey began when I determined that I would genuinely love and respect every Christian who came into my life, not just those I already agreed with or who identified with my group. I looked around at each Christian I encountered and asked myself, how should I share my life with them in the Spirit? This required nothing less than a new lifestyle. My prayer life was altered immediately. I consciously tracked my relationships with new awareness and actually began to ask God to bring a wide diversity of Christians into my daily experience.

There is growing evidence that many Christians are deeply concerned about our disunity, and a growing number of them are beginning to get a vision of unity in mission. This is evident in international and national conferences, the genuine renewal of transdenominational ministerial associations, city-wide prayer movements, vibrant expressions of compassion for the weakest and poorest who live on the margins of modern society, schools that have begun to grasp the unity factor and clearly teach it, and so forth. The "what now" question can be answered best when we seek fresh ways to pray together, work together, break bread together, and love and trust one another. By these personal, sacrificial efforts, we can begin to conceive of a more united church regardless of the varied forms that the church might take. We can then seriously address the racial, ethnic, and gender divisions that still profoundly harm our witness to the world.

I believe the vision we need to grasp is one of *visible unity in reconciled diversity*. It just might be that we need more diversity, not less. More diversity would actually offer us even greater opportunity to truly listen, love, and serve in the supernatural love of Jesus. It would also offer the widest opportunity for the world to see how we truly love one another. Sameness and success are not our aim. The unity factor requires not only a radical shift in our thinking but a whole new understanding of how unity releases our shared energies as our collective resources are used for the common good. I am seeing a plethora of models emerge and believe there are many more to come.

What would it look like, for example, if your church and/or mission began to take seriously the biblical mandate to serve and honor others first? What if the goal were not to grow *your* church and/or mission first but to build up *Christ's* church in love and peace? Writing to the whole church in Rome, which gathered in a number of different homes and places, Paul said, "Love must be sincere. Hate what is evil; cling to what is good. Be devoted to one another in love. Honor one another above yourselves" (Rom. 12:9–10).

If we embrace the unity factor that I have described, we can then pursue the following commitments together:

1. We can deepen our commitment to Christ, the gospel, and the mission that we have in the world by intentionally working with other Christians and churches.

2. We can work together to enhance our understanding of the diversity of our mission while we variously serve the same end—namely, the glory of Christ.

3. We can pursue principles and practices that will enable us to act responsibly and peaceably with our Christian brothers and sisters who hold to different views of Scripture and reflect distinctive models of the church.

4. We can engage in deeper theological reflection in areas where we share genuine mutual concern. These are much more numerous than we have seen. This will help us do a better job of being faithful to Christ and our neighbors.

5. We can strengthen the wholeness of the entire church in our city or region by engaging in honest communication, intercessory prayer for one another, and partnership wherever possible.

6. We can foster relationships that will actually lead us into every opportunity that we can find for common witness to the whole world.[1]

Several years ago, one of our premier theologians was asked what *all* Christians could do *together*. He said there were two things that we must do and no church excludes any of us from doing them. First, we can read the Holy Scripture together. We can learn from Jesus and consider how his life fills and forms our relationships. Second, we can pray together. We can actually talk to God and one another in Christ-centered prayer. Consider this counsel in the light of what I have written. It is so simple, yet so profound.

If unity is rooted in *relational love*, then we must build trust before we can share in mission. We cannot build trust without hearing God's Word and sharing in response to it in prayer. It is past time for this to happen on a wide and growing scale. This effort will almost never bear instant results. Maybe this is one reason we find this work so frustrating. We would much rather find programs that will make unity happen. Remember, Jesus called us first to "love one another" and then to love the world.

Do not get me wrong. Programs and planning have their place in putting the unity factor into practice. However, until we are deeply and personally convinced of the truth of the unity factor, we will never invest our lives in deep, lasting relationships that bring solutions to our present division.

---

1. These points have been freely adapted from the "Guiding Purpose Statement" of the Global Christian Forum, adopted in 2002 in Pasadena, California.

Finally, we must realize that the unity factor is about real discipleship. Furthermore, we must understand that real discipleship is *not* about scholarship or formal teaching, as important as both are for training the minds of leaders. The critical disciplines of true discipleship teach us to be like Christ in love and humility; to *think* about biblical truths in abstract ways. Thus, the cost of real discipleship is always very high. Only those deeply convinced of this divinely given solution to our disunity will offer themselves as a "living sacrifice, holy and pleasing to God—this is your true and proper worship" (Rom. 12:1).

We must understand that true discipleship involves every nook and cranny of our life. For millions of people, Christianity is a religious activity they give a little of their time to on Sunday morning. They have some measure of faith, but discipleship means little or nothing to them.

> The withering of discipleship is one of the gravest threats facing the church today. The main cause is that churches have disconnected discipleship from everyday life. Too often, pastors talk about "our walk with God" and "stewardship" almost exclusively in terms of formally religious activities such as worship attendance, Bible study, evangelism, and giving. As crucial as these activities are for every Christian, they will never take up more than a tiny percentage of life for those who are not in full-time ministry. The largest portion of life—our work in the home and in our jobs—is excluded from our concept of discipleship and stewardship. This leaves us preaching a faith that is not relevant to the totality of people's lives.[2]

The Cape Town Commitment expressed the idea of whole-life discipleship well by adding, "[whole-life discipleship means] *to live, think, work, and speak from a biblical worldview and with missional effectiveness in every place or circumstance of daily life*

---

2. Lester DeKoster, *Work: The Meaning of Your Life*, 2d ed. (Grand Rapids: Christian's Library Press, 2010), 63.

and work" (italics mine).[3] Nothing less is needed if we are serious about missional-ecumenism.

Plainly put, the mission of Christ has been entrusted to all of Christ's disciples, not just to clergy and professional missionaries. Every day, in every way, the gospel is best spread through the lives of those who are salt and light in their families, neighborhoods, cities, and workplaces. No church program can accomplish this mission. The call to whole-life discipleship is revolutionary in the modern West. When we begin to grasp whole-life discipleship, and people start to live it out, things will change. The unity factor will play a major role in this change.

Let us be honest. Our churches need a whole new culture, one not rooted in individualism, but in this profoundly New Testament understanding. Face it, Christ did not come to earth to live for thirty-plus years, die on the cross, descend into the grave, rise on the third day, and ascend into heaven to merely provide for a private salvation lived out in our hearts alone. Our leaders need both wisdom and holy courage to make this clear and to help us pursue the new church culture that we desperately need in these complex times. The wind of God's Spirit is blowing, and many are responding. Will *you* become an active part of the solution by embracing the unity factor and putting it into practice in all your relationships?

We must understand that the unity of the church is not an end in itself. Unity is a sign and an instrument of the first fruits of God's purpose to reconcile all things in heaven and on earth through Jesus Christ. By faith, we already enjoy a foretaste of the end. Unity is a sign that leads us to experience the foretaste of the divine purpose. Jesus is the end for which all things were made (Col. 1:15–20). This is precisely why unity matters so profoundly (Col. 3:1–4; 12–17).

I have argued that the unity factor means all Christians have one Lord, they belong to one church, and together they should

---

3. *The Cape Town Commitment*, 36.

share in Christ's one (kingdom) mission. However, what does this mean for you?

If Jesus is Lord, then nothing is more important than your *personal relationship* with him. If you resonate with the unity factor, then you should seek personal renewal (Matt. 22:34–40). This is not a one-time event but a disciplined process. With the psalmist, you must long for God as a deer pants for daily water (Ps. 42:1). This requires time spent in God's presence, particularly times of contemplation and quiet where the struggles of life are truly won. (For many of you, this will require a period of time dedicated to solitude where you turn off media and social networking.) If you will not intentionally draw near to Jesus in private, then all the efforts you make for unity and mission will come to mean nothing.

If the church is one, then we must live life forward in a deeply relational oneness. What we do together matters far more than our lone-ranger choices. This is why the New Testament is filled with encouragements to share with one another. Until you live the Christian life in faith, hope, and love—building trust with your brothers and sisters who belong to the same Lord—you will never know the unity I speak about. Two people can be united in death, even sharing the same grave. The unity we must have is not one shared in death but in life. It is nothing less than the life-giving presence of Jesus among us.

Finally, if we share one mission, then we must follow Jesus *together*. We must love and serve the world in the name and fellowship of the one who is Lord. This will require us to form creative *partnerships* that are deeply personal, partnerships that will take us beyond the denominational barriers that have been nurtured by pride and mistrust.

We all are one in mission,
We all are one in call,
Our varied gifts united
By Christ, the Lord of all.
A single, great commission
Compels us from above
To plan and work together
That all may know Christ's love.

We all are called to service
To witness in God's name;
Our ministries are different,
Our purpose is the same:
To touch the lives of others
With God's surprising grace
So ev'ry folk and nation
May feel God's warm embrace.

Now let us be united
And let our song be heard.
Now let us be a vessel
For God's redeeming word.
We all are one in mission,
We all are one in call,
Our varied gifts united
By Christ, the Lord of all.[4]

---

4. Rusty Edwards. Copyright Hope Publishing Company, 1986. Arrangement copyright Augsburg Fortress, 1992. Music a Finnish folk tune of the nineteenth century. See *With One Voice*, Augsburg Fortress, 1995, hymn 755.

ABOUT THE AUTHORS

JOHN H. ARMSTRONG is the president and founder of ACT 3 (Advancing the Christian Tradition in the Third Millennium) in Carol Stream, Illinois. He has extensive speaking and consulting experience in many contexts and Christian denominations. He served as a pastor for more than twenty years. He is an adjunct professor of evangelism at Wheaton College Graduate School and has taught as a guest at many colleges and seminaries. He is the author or editor of twelve books and thousands of blogs and online articles available at www.act3online.com.

Through the mission of ACT 3, John equips leaders for unity in Christ's mission. He does this through intensive cohort-based training that focuses on the key principles of missional-ecumenism as taught in *The Unity Factor*. The vision is to shape a new kind of leadership that reflects the teaching of Jesus in both thought and practice. The ultimate goal is to create a growing nucleus of world-changing leaders who will intentionally invest their lives in the kingdom of God. Information about these cohort-based groups is available at www.act3online.com.

TIMOTHY GEORGE is the founding dean of Beeson Divinity School of Samford University in Birmingham, Alabama, and general editor of the *Reformation Commentary on Scripture* published by InterVarsity Press.

Christian's **|||LIBRARY PRESS**

Founded in 1979 by Gerard Berghoef and Lester DeKoster, **CHRISTIAN'S LIBRARY PRESS** has been committed to publishing influential texts on church leadership, the vocation of work, and stewardship for more than thirty years. During that time Berghoef and DeKoster wrote significant works including *The Deacons Handbook*, *The Elders Handbook*, and *God's Yardstick*, which still are in demand today. After the passing of Lester DeKoster in 2009, the imprint is now administered by the Acton Institute for the Study of Religion & Liberty. For more information about Christian's Library Press, visit www.clpress.com.

ACTONINSTITUTE

With its commitment to pursue a society that is free and virtuous, the **ACTON INSTITUTE FOR THE STUDY OF RELIGION & LIBERTY** is a leading voice in the international environmental and social policy debate. With offices in Grand Rapids, Michigan, and Rome, Italy, as well as affiliates in four other nations around the world, the Acton Institute is uniquely positioned to comment on the sound economic and moral foundations necessary to sustain humane environmental and social policies. The Acton Institute is a nonprofit, ecumenical think tank working internationally to "promote a free and virtuous society characterized by individual liberty and sustained by religious principles." For more on the Acton Institute, please visit www.acton.org.

ACT 3

ACT 3 is a ministry to equip leaders for unity in Christ's mission.

ACT 3 is deeply committed to enabling Christian leaders to exegete both culture and Scripture in order to speak into our present context in ways that are faithful to the missional purposes of God as revealed in Holy Scripture. We do this by teaching leaders how to connect Jesus' prayer for unity (John 17) with his commission to make disciples of all nations (Matthew 28).

We express this purpose through four core convictions:

Missional Character of the Church

We believe that the life and witness of the church should be thoroughly shaped by its participation in the mission of God to reconcile the world to himself in Jesus Christ, and by the call of Jesus to be the people of God sent into the world to proclaim and live out the gospel.

Primacy of Scripture

We believe that Scripture is inspired by God and as such is infallible and authoritative for the life and witness of the church throughout history and across cultures.

Indispensable Significance of the Christian Tradition

We affirm the summary of Christian faith taught in the Apostles' Creed and the Nicene Creed and are committed to seeking wisdom from the history and traditions of the one, holy, catholic and apostolic church.

Necessity of Cultural Engagement

We are committed to ongoing engagement with culture and the world for the sake of our unified witness to the gospel and continual learning from Christians in other cultural settings.

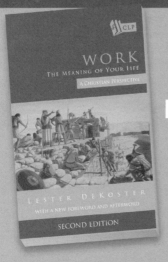

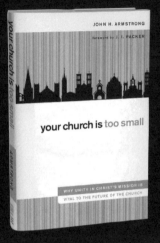

"That all of them may be ONE..."

- John 17:21

This book is a must-read for anyone who has grown weary with Christian divisiveness and schism and longs to discover ways of strengthening the bonds that unite us in the Spirit of Christ."

— Chuck Colson